DOG ON A BIKE!

And More True Stories of Amazing Animal Talents!

Moira Rose Donohue

NATIONAL
GEOGRAPHIC

WASHINGTON, D.C.

Since 1888, the National Geographic Society has
funded more than 12,000 research, exploration, and
preservation projects around the world. The Society
receives funds from National Geographic Partners,
LLC, funded in part by your purchase. A portion of
the proceeds from this book supports this vital work.
To learn more, visit natgeo.com/info.

NATIONAL GEOGRAPHIC and Yellow Border
Design are trademarks of the National Geographic
Society, used under license.

For more information, visit nationalgeographic.com,
call 1-800-647-5463, or write to the following address:

National Geographic Partners
1145 17th Street N.W.
Washington, D.C. 20036-4688 U.S.A.

Visit us online at nationalgeographic.com/books

For librarians and teachers: ngchildrensbooks.org

More for kids from National Geographic:
kids.nationalgeographic.com

For information about special discounts for bulk
purchases, please contact National Geographic Books
Special Sales: specialsales@natgeo.com

For rights or permissions inquiries, please contact
National Geographic Books Subsidiary Rights:
bookrights@natgeo.com

Art directed by Sanjida Rashid
Designed by Ruth Ann Thompson

National Geographic supports K–12
educators with ELA Common Core
Resources. Visit natgeoed.org/
commoncore for more information.

Trade paperback ISBN: 978-1-4263-2705-6
Reinforced library edition ISBN: 978-1-4263-2706-3

Printed in China
16/RRDS/1

Table of CONTENTS

Is that a dog on a bike? Yes! It's Norman.

NORMAN:
DOG
ON A BIKE!

Norman takes a spin around the block.

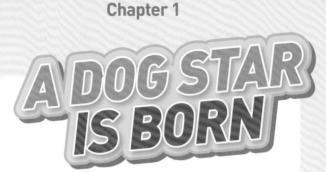

Chapter 1

A DOG STAR IS BORN

Something is moving at the end of the block. And it's coming closer. Is it a bear on skates? A Wookie on wheels? No, it's Norman, a Briard (sounds like bree-ARD). And he's riding a bike!

What's a Briard? It's a very shaggy dog. The breed came from France. But Norman isn't just any Briard. He's a superstar dog.

Norman can ride a bike all by himself. He hangs his fuzzy front paws over the handlebars. Then he pushes the pedals with his back feet. And off he goes, fur flying! True, the bike still has training wheels. But he's not even six years old yet!

It all started years ago. Norman is owned by Karen Cobb. She's a professional (sounds like pro-FESH-eh-nahl) dog trainer. Her father was a vet, so she grew up around animals. But she never had her own pet dog. After she finished college, Karen got a dog of her own. It was a Shiba Inu (sounds like SHEE-buh EE-noo). She wanted him to be very well trained. So she read every dog

Did You Know?

Briards come from the Brie region of France. The Brie region is also known for its world-famous cheese!

training book she could find. She took classes, and she began teaching him.

She didn't know it, but Shiba Inus pick and choose which commands they obey. That makes them hard to train. Teaching him basic obedience (sounds like oh-BEE-DEE-ens) skills, like "come" and "watch," was a challenge. It was also difficult to teach him agility skills, like running through a tunnel and weaving between poles. But she kept working at it. Eventually, he came in first place for his breed in the entire country!

Karen was hooked on dog training. She wanted to do it for her job. So she took more classes and worked at a dog training company. That's when she first met a Briard named Norman. Norman's owners wanted Karen to train him.

Briards are big, lovable oafs. They weigh about 75 pounds (34 kg). They have long, wavy fur. Some have ears that stand up. They love to jump and bounce. Briards are herding dogs. They stay very close to their owners. That makes them easy to train. And although they often act like clowns, these goofballs are supersmart and very loyal. Karen wanted to own one. But by then, she had two Shiba Inus. She would have to wait to get another dog.

Karen opened her own dog training school. She had a busy life with her family, her business, and her dogs. Finally, after many years, she knew it was the right time to get a Briard. She researched all the breeders and found the one she liked best. This breeder was in Washington State,

U.S.A. Karen called her.

"I want a dog that is gentle but one that really wants to learn," she told the breeder. The breeder understood.

But she said it might be a while. That was OK. Karen was willing to wait until just the right litter came along. After all, it's not every day that a star is born.

In fact, it took another year and a half before the breeder thought she had the right litter of pups. Karen flew out to meet the puppies. There were four that were "show quality." That means they could compete in dog shows. The breeder put different-colored collars on those four so that Karen could identify them.

"Here, fetch!" Karen said as she threw toys to the four pups. She watched to see who wanted to play.

Then she ran and hid. She waited to see who would come to find her. Two pups did. They seemed to be the most curious. But the one with the blue collar was gentler.

"Come here, boy," she said. He bounded up to her. She ruffled his fluffy fur. Karen knew then that he was the one. It had been a long wait, but worth it. Can you guess what she named him? Norman, after the first Briard in her life!

Norman was about to begin his new life with Karen. But first, he had to travel to Georgia, U.S.A., where Karen lived. It was almost 2,000 miles (3,219 km) away. He would have to fly on a plane.

Someone to Watch Over Me

Herding dogs are bred to work on farms and ranches. They move livestock from one place to another. They can make sheep and cattle head in the right direction. They bark and chase them around. And when that doesn't work, they nip them. German shepherds are herding dogs. So are border collies and, of course, Briards. Corgis (sounds like KOR-geese) herd, too, even though they are only about one foot (30.5 cm) tall at the shoulder. Herding dogs are smart and make good pets. But sometimes they try to herd their owners!

Karen spent two days getting Norman ready for his big adventure. She got a soft, nylon dog carrier bag. It had mesh on some of the sides so he could see out and breathe easily. To make him more comfortable, she put him in the carrier for longer and longer periods. After a little while, he got used to being inside.

Karen also began his obedience training. To teach "sit" and "down," Karen used a technique called luring (sounds like LURH-ing). Here's how it worked.

Karen held a treat in her hand. Then she moved the treat in the direction she wanted Norman to move. She used the command words and hand signals. That way he got two different clues about what she wanted. When he got it right, she rewarded him with a treat.

Norman learned these commands fast. So fast that after only two days that smart little pup knew three basic commands by heart!

Karen took Norman to the airport. While they were waiting to board the plane, she worked on his training. Norman was only eight weeks old, but he wanted to learn.

When it came time for their flight, Karen gently coaxed Norman into his carrier. He wasn't afraid. They boarded the plane. Karen placed Norman's carrier under the seat in front of her. Their life together was about to start!

Norman the pup tries driving a car.

Chapter 2

HOT DOGGING IT!

During the flight, Karen worried about how long Norman would have to wait before he could go to the bathroom. Puppies usually have to go potty every few hours. Karen had a clever idea. She took Norman into the bathroom on the plane. She put puppy pads on the floor. But Norman wasn't interested.

After they landed, Karen and Norman drove home from the airport. Norman still hadn't gone to the bathroom. It's not healthy for a puppy to hold it that long. Karen was getting worried. She let him out of the car. Norman sniffed around. Finally, he found the right spot. It had been 15 hours. What a good dog!

"OK, everyone, meet Norman," said Karen. Her husband, son, and daughter rushed up to meet the little pup. He bounced from one person to the next. He licked their noses. They offered him some puppy food. But Norman didn't want to eat. And he wasn't ready for bed. Karen couldn't believe it. He wanted to work.

So she grabbed some treats. She started training Norman right then and there. She taught him a new command. When he got it right, he got a treat!

Many dog owners stop training after they teach a dog "sit," "stay," and "come." But Karen knew that Norman wanted to learn a lot more than that. She taught him to push open the back door from the outside. Then she trained him to close the door behind him. Finally, she taught him to wipe his feet!

Wiping his feet was one of the hardest tricks for him. To teach him, Karen put a treat under a rug. She waited for him to scratch the rug to get the treat. Then she said, "Wipe your feet!" It took a couple of weeks to learn to do it on command. But it can take some people longer than that!

Next, Norman was ready to begin his agility training. He learned to run obstacle (sounds like AHB-stuh-cuhl) courses. He was quite a sight tearing through tunnels and leaping over fences with his long fur streaming.

Karen also tried to teach him fancier tricks. She used "shaping." She waited for him to do something she thought was cute. Then she gave him a reward. She gave his trick a name. Every time he did it again, he got another treat.

Karen also used a clicker when she trained Norman. A clicker is a small piece of metal that makes a clicking noise. She clicked it as soon as Norman did something right. Then she gave him a treat. The clicker is a good way to let a dog know which behavior he did correctly.

Norman moved on to tricks that are used by dogs in movies. This is called "studio training." It takes a very smart dog to learn how to act in a movie. The first thing they learn is to "hit a mark." That means they have to walk to a spot marked on the floor and stop. Next, Karen showed Norman how to turn right and left. She also taught him to tilt his head on cue. When he did, he looked like he was curious about something. He even learned to "dock dive." That means he ran off a dock and jumped into the water!

Basic Training

Teaching a dog basic commands helps owners control and protect their dogs. Here are some easy ways to train your dog:

Sit—Get on your dog's level. Hold a treat close to his nose. Move it up slowly. As his head follows it, his bottom will hit the floor. Give him the treat and praise him. Do it again, and say "Sit!"

Come—Put a leash on the dog. Face your dog and start walking backward. When the dog comes to you, give him a treat and say "Come!"

Every now and then Norman would get tired. He would bite at his leash to say *Stop! I need a break.* But that didn't happen often.

Norman was also the family's pet. Right from the start, he slept on Karen's bed. Unlike most dogs, Norman slept on his back. What a sight—this big, shaggy dog with his paws stuck up in the air!

Norman loved to play with the family. When they sat on the couch, Norman ran to find a toy. Tail wagging, he would drop it in front of the couch. *Fetch, anyone?* Sometimes he brought a rope toy. He nudged the kids. Surely someone would play his favorite game—tug!

At Christmastime, the family put wrapped presents under the tree. Norman never touched them until Christmas morning. But one year, Karen's son had a friend over. They exchanged presents a few days early. Norman saw them tearing off the wrapping paper. He dove under the tree. Somehow that brainy Briard knew which presents were his. He found one and tore it open!

One day, Karen took her children to the playground. Norman went with them. Karen let him off his leash. The children climbed up the ladder to the slide. Norman climbed up, too! Uh-oh! How was he going to get down? On the slide, of course. Paws first!

Another time, Karen's children were riding on scooters in the backyard. Norman bounded up and sniffed one of the scooters and wagged his tail.

"Do you want to ride that?" Karen asked Norman. She held the scooter up. She helped him hook his big fluffy paws over the handlebars. Then, all by himself, Norman put one paw down. Karen clicked, which meant "Good dog!" She did that every time he put his paw down. Then, over time, she showed him how to push with his paw. It took a while, but Norman did it. Before long, Norman was scootering down the block on a pink princess scooter with rainbow handlebar ribbons!

In 2011, David Letterman, who hosted a famous TV show, heard about Norman the Scooter Dog. He liked to have talented animals on his show. He invited Karen and Norman to come to New York City.

Superstar Norman
poses on Broadway.

WHO LET THE DOGS OUT?

Karen and Norman stayed in a fancy hotel in New York. Some famous people were staying there, too. Reporters were nearby. They were waiting for the celebrities (sounds like suh-LEH-brih-teez) to come out of the hotel.

"Come on, Norman, let's practice," said Karen. Norman rode his scooter in front of the hotel. The reporters saw Norman on his scooter.

They loved it. So they filmed him. The next day, videos of Norman were all over the news and the Internet. People were amazed. And overnight, Norman was a star!

Norman's life changed. A pet food company wanted to hire him. Everyone wanted to see him ride his scooter. But Karen had a problem. She and her husband had been saving money for three years. They planned to take a nine-month family trip across the country and Canada. They were leaving as soon as she and Norman got back from New York.

Karen didn't want the family to miss out on this dream trip. But she wanted Norman to have his chance on TV. *What should they do?* Karen thought about it. She decided that they should go on the trip.

But Karen talked to the pet food company. They were happy to set up tapings at TV news stations along the way. In the end, Norman appeared on dozens of shows!

While they were traveling, they got a phone call. It was from a dog reality show. The show was called *Who Let the Dogs Out?* The show wanted Norman to costar with a bulldog named Tillman.

This is Norman's big chance, Karen thought. So they cut the trip a little short. And Norman and Karen stayed in California to film the show.

Karen drove Norman everywhere. He hadn't been on a

Did You Know?

In 2006, a greyhound named Cinderella May set a world record for the highest jump by a dog. She leaped 68 inches (172.7 cm) into the air!

plane since she brought him home as a puppy. But now, Norman would have to travel by plane to different cities for each of the tapings.

Karen didn't want him to travel in the cargo area of the plane like most pets. No worries! Now he was an "animal celebrity." That meant he got his very own seat—in first class! Karen enjoyed her first-class seat. But Norman curled up on the floor.

Soon Norman was ready for a new challenge. And he got one. Guinness World Records contacted Karen. They wondered if Norman would like to try to set the world record for the fastest

Did You Know?

The world record for the longest tail is held by an Irish wolfhound named Finnegan. His tail is more than two feet (72.29 cm) long!

30

dog on a scooter. They told Karen to let them know if she was interested.

"Oh, yes," said Karen. She and Norman practiced at home. On July 12, 2013, Norman and Karen arrived at the course. Norman hopped up on his scooter. But then he jumped off. Was he nervous?

There were cameras and people everywhere. But he had been on lots of TV shows. He was used to it. He stepped on again. This time he started to push. Karen walked in front of him. "Come on, Norman," she said. "You've got this."

Norman pushed harder. Then he coasted for a second and pushed again. Would it be enough? Karen held her breath.

Norman glided to the finish line. People cheered and whistled. Norman hopped off.

He bounced up and down. Karen hugged him. He had done it!

Norman rode 100 feet (just over 30 m). And he did it in 20.77 seconds. He had set a new world record.

Norman had done a lot. But he wasn't finished. Karen discovered something important about Norman. He needed to learn a new task or he would get bored. She looked around her house, trying to get ideas of what to teach him next. Then she knew. She would teach him how to ride a bike!

This was trickier than riding a scooter. He would have to learn how to push the pedals. To get him started, Karen put him on a stationary (sounds like STAY-shun-air-ee) bike. That's a bike that can't move, like an exercise bike.

Briards in Hollywood

Briards were bred
to protect their herds
against attack. Then they were
used to move livestock around, like other
herding dogs. During World War I, they
helped find wounded soldiers. Today they
are often used in TV shows. That's
because they are so smart. It makes
them easy to train. Look closely the next
time you see a big, shaggy, lovable dog
on TV. It may have long ears or it may
have ears that stand up. Either way,
there's a good chance it's a Briard!

When Norman put his foot on a pedal, Karen clicked her clicker. That let him know he was doing what she wanted him to do. When he moved the pedal, she would click again. Eventually he was ready to try it on a regular bike. They used training wheels so he would stay balanced.

It's a big moment when a kid rides a bike for the first time. It's even bigger when a dog does it! Norman enjoyed riding his bike. He got better at it. And he went faster.

Karen wanted to see if Norman was fast enough to set another world record. This time it would take place on TV. On July 5, 2014, he set the world record. He pedaled 100 feet (30 meters) in 55.41 seconds! That's like going from one base to another on a baseball diamond in less than a minute.

Norman has starred in TV shows and ads. He holds two world records. And in 2016, he won the World Dog Award for Top Trick for his bike riding!

Has fame changed him? Well, he thinks everyone should pet him and pay attention to him. Of course, a lot of dogs *without* his talent think that, too!

It seems like there's nothing this talented dog can't learn. But here's a secret—there is one thing. Norman loves to swim. And he gets upset if someone jumps in a swimming pool when he isn't allowed in. He makes a high-pitched squeal to let Karen know that he wants to jump in, too. And no matter what Karen does, she can't make him stop squealing!

Eddie the otter takes his sport seriously.

EDDIE: SLAM DUNK SEA OTTER!

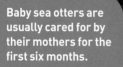

Baby sea otters are usually cared for by their mothers for the first six months.

Chapter 1

BETWEEN A ROCK AND A HARD PLACE

One spring day, the Marine Mammal Center in northern California, U.S.A, got a phone call. The center helps sea animals that are hurt or sick. The phone call was from people walking on Moonstone Beach. They had found a baby sea otter on the sand. They put him near a large rock. It sheltered him from the sun and wind.

Workers from the center jumped in a truck. They rushed to the beach. They found the stranded pup. He was tiny and weak.

Squeak, squeak, squeak! he whined.

The marine center workers scooped him up. He was too young to be alone. Mother sea otters take care of their pups until they are five or six months old. Mothers swim on their backs. They snuggle their babies on their tummies.

The workers guessed this pup was about five weeks old. Somehow he had gotten separated from his mother. They took the frightened pup back to the center. They kept him warm and gave him liquids. They saved the little otter's life.

Sea otters are part of the weasel family. Weasels are small mammals. Many weasels have long, thin bodies. Most live on land, like ferrets and the honey badger.

But sea otters live in the water. They are born to swim. Their back feet are webbed and look like flippers.

This little guy had been out of the water for a while. The workers were worried about him because he was alone. So they took him to the Monterey Bay Aquarium (sounds like uh-KWAIR-ee-um). A vet there examined him. The baby otter was going to be OK. But he needed to be taken care of. The aquarium already had a lot of otters that needed help. They didn't have room for one more.

So the staff from the marine center took the pup to their main office. They named him Eddie. They fed him formula from a bottle every two hours. It was a lot of work. But otters need to eat a lot. Sea otters grow to about four feet (1.2 m) long. They weigh about 65 pounds (29 kg). They eat at least 25 percent of their weight every day. That's a lot of food!

Eddie lived in his own pen at the center. It had a pool in the middle filled with sea water. He could pop in and out of the water. Sea otters don't have layers of fat to keep them warm in the water like whales do. Instead, they have two layers of fur. The top layer is long and waterproof. The thick fur underneath traps the air. That protects the otter from the cold water.

Mother sea otters teach their babies how to groom themselves. It's not that they want to look pretty. They comb their fur with their paws to keep air near their skin. That keeps them warm. Eddie didn't know how to do this. Every time he went into the water, the people at the center had to brush and comb his fur.

After two months, the Monterey Bay Aquarium finally had room for Eddie. That's when he met Thelma. Thelma was a sea otter who had been rescued a couple of weeks after Eddie. Thelma and Eddie would become best friends. Eddie met other sea otters as well. The workers were hoping he would learn from them how to behave like an otter. But Eddie had been around people for most of his short life. He paid more attention to humans than to other otters. The staff didn't think they could return him to the wild.

They thought Thelma might have a chance of being released, though. She had been with other sea otters since she was rescued. In November, the aquarium turned her loose in the ocean and waited to see what would happen.

Wild sea otters live along the Pacific coast. They learn how to find food from their mothers. They usually look for dinner close to shore where the water is shallow. But they can hold their breath for five minutes. So they can also dive deep. Then they search for sea urchins, mussels, and clams along the bottom of the ocean. They dig them out of the sand with their strong front paws.

After two days, workers from the aquarium checked on Thelma. They saw

The underfur of a sea otter is dense. It can have as many as one million hairs per square inch (6 square cm). A human has only about 100,000 hairs in total on his or her head!

her taking food from a fisherman. She wasn't finding food on her own! So they picked her up and brought her back to the aquarium. They released her again a month later. But she still wasn't finding food by herself. So they took her back to the aquarium for good.

Meanwhile, a zoo in Oregon wanted to set up a sea otter exhibit. The director of the zoo wrote a letter to the aquarium. *The Oregon Zoo is looking for otters that can't be returned to the ocean,* he told them. The aquarium told him about Thelma and Eddie. The zoo director was excited. But first he had to talk to the U. S. government.

The "Other" Otter

There are 13 different kinds of otters in the world. But only two live in North America. They are the river otter and the sea otter. River otters live in freshwater. They are smaller than sea otters. They tip the scales at only 25 pounds (11 kg). River otters spend half their time on land. They can run quickly on their little paws. River otters are playful rascals. And unlike sea otters, who eat their food off their bellies, river otters dine on top of rocks or logs.

Many years ago, sea otters were hunted for their fur. Too many of them were killed off. So the government made laws to protect them.

The government said the zoo could take both otters. But the exhibit at the zoo wasn't ready yet. Thelma and Eddie would have to go someplace else first. A zoo in Tacoma, Washington, offered to take the young pups. They sent a private plane to pick up the otters.

Eddie and Thelma lived at the Washington zoo for about a year. They liked to be with each other. They floated on their backs and held each other's paws. Sea otters do that so they stay close to one another in the water.

Thelma accepts a treat from one of the trainers.

In the summer of 2000, the Oregon Zoo exhibit was ready. The zoo was excited to have Eddie and Thelma. They were the zoo's first sea otters ever! The zoo wanted to welcome its newest animals. So the trainers gave the otters lots of toys and treats. They filled hard hats with crabs. They stuck mussels inside tubes. They let the otters play in piles of ice. *Brrrrr!*

But Eddie and Thelma weren't going to live a life of leisure (sounds like LEE-zhur). The zookeepers had other ideas. They were going to train the otters! Sea otters are very smart. They use tools. Very few mammals can do that.

For example, sea otters can pry a rock from the ocean floor. When they catch a clam, they lie on their backs. They hold the clam on their bellies. *Kakakak! Kakakak!* They smash the shell open with the rock. They dig out the tasty morsel inside! If they find a rock they really like, they hide it in a secret "pocket" of skin under their arms for next time.

Because otters are so smart, they're easy to train. It turned out that Eddie was especially quick to learn. Most of his training taught him skills that would help the zookeepers take care of him. But first, they trained him to go to his spot. That meant he had to swim to a special rock in the exhibit. Once he was separate from the other otters, the trainers could work with him.

They trained Eddie to open his mouth. Then they could brush his teeth. They showed him how to get on a scale so they could weigh him.

They also wanted to give Eddie exercise. Sea otters would make great gymnasts! They are very flexible. They can twist and bend. They turn somersaults (sounds like SUMMER-salts) with ease. The zookeepers taught Eddie to do this on cue. It helped him stay fit. And it was a good challenge for him mentally.

One of the ways they trained him was by using a target stick. First, the trainer would say "Target," and touch Eddie's nose with a pole. "Good boy," the trainer would say. Then Eddie would get a treat—maybe a tasty shrimp or a clam.

Then the trainer would do it again and again. Pretty soon Eddie would touch the pole on his own when a trainer said "Target." Now the trainers could move the pole and say "Target." Eddie would follow and touch the pole. They could ask Eddie to swim in different directions. It wasn't long before he would twist and turn on cue.

Superheroes of the Sea

Sea urchins are spiny animals that live in the ocean. They gobble up kelp. Kelp is a type of seaweed. It's food and shelter for many other sea animals. And it protects beaches from wearing down. Sea urchins can destroy the kelp forests. That's where the sea otters come in. They help keep the balance by feasting on the urchins. That saves the sea kelp for others. And that's why sea otters are called a "keystone species." It means they play a very important role in their ecosystem.

Sea otters are curious. So it's important to keep them active and busy. Eddie was so curious that the trainers had to think of lots of things to teach him. They taught him to spin in the water. They taught him to put his paws up when they asked. And they asked him to fetch things and bring them back. They would be glad they taught him that later.

The trainers sometimes asked Eddie to perform his tricks for zoo visitors. They would ask him to swim up to the glass. Then he would open his mouth or put his little paws up! People couldn't help smiling at him. Eddie went from being an orphan to being one of the zoo's stars!

In 2011, Jenny DeGroot started working at the zoo. She was the lead sea otter keeper. Jenny grew up in Chicago, Illinois, U.S.A. When she was a little girl, she went to the zoo in Chicago. She watched the dolphins and walruses. Her best friend had a pool in her backyard. Jenny and her friend would take turns pretending to be the dolphin and the trainer! Jenny knew that when she grew up, she wanted to work with marine mammals.

Did You Know?

A group of otters floating in the water is called a raft.

Jenny studied marine biology (sounds like by-AH-loh-gee). Her first job was at an aquarium. Then she moved to Alaska, U.S.A. She worked at a marine center there. That's where she began to work with sea otter pups that had been stranded. She fell in love with this

kind of work.
Now, she
would work
with sea otters
in Oregon.
Soon after she
arrived at the Oregon Zoo,
Jenny saw that Eddie's eyes were
swollen. She asked the vet to look at him.
The vet told her that Eddie had a disease
in his eyes. He needed eye drops. But how
would she give eye drops to a sea otter?

Jenny decided to use Eddie's "head
cage." That's a small square of fencing
just big enough for Eddie's head. He was
already trained to put his head in this cage
so they could examine him. Jenny would
have to teach Eddie to keep his head in the

cage long enough for her to give him his eye drops.

Jenny decided to use the pole and the word "Target." She moved the pole so Eddie would tilt his head up. When he moved his head the right way, she gave him a treat. Next she showed him the eye dropper. She didn't want him to be afraid of it. She drizzled water from the dropper into the cage. She did this for several days. Finally, after he was used to it, she squirted medicine into his eyes. He stayed still for it and kept his eyes open. He knew a big treat was coming. Sure enough, Jenny gave him one of his favorites—a tasty shrimp! It didn't take long before Eddie took his eye drops every time.

Eddie rarely misses a shot. Two points!

Chapter 3

GOT GAME?

When Jenny joined the zoo, Eddie was already 13 years old. Sea otters can live 23 years in the wild. But they usually live between 10 and 12 years. At 13, Eddie wasn't a young pup anymore. In fact, he was getting old. He was having some health problems.

The vets wanted to take an x-ray of Eddie to give him a full checkup.

To get a good x-ray, a patient must lie very still. Animals are often given a medication that makes them sleepy before an x-ray. That way they won't move. But Jenny knew it would be better for Eddie if he could learn to be still without any medicine. Then the doctors could take the x-ray photos while he was awake.

Using the target pole, Jenny trained Eddie to lie underneath a table with an x-ray machine on top. He didn't seem to mind. And he was willing to stay there long enough for the x-ray pictures to be taken. The vets looked at the x-rays. And they discovered that Eddie had arthritis (sounds like arth-RITE-us). That's a disease of the joints. Eddie had it in his elbows. They wanted him to exercise his arms. It would help him feel better.

How am I going to do that? Jenny wondered. Swimming sometimes helps people with arthritis. But that wouldn't help Eddie. Sea otters don't use their front paws to swim. So she needed something else. Then she got an idea. She would teach him how to play basketball!

Luckily, Eddie already knew how to fetch things and bring them to the trainer. That's how she would start his training. Jenny picked out a new ball for him. That would show him that it was a new trick. The ball was orange, like a basketball. But it was only about the size of a melon. She tossed it into the water.

See Otter?

What should you do if you come across a sea otter on land? First, don't touch it. Otters can carry diseases. And they can hurt you, especially if they are scared. So ask someone to guard the otter. He or she can keep dogs and other animals away. Then call your local animal control. Be ready to tell the people on the phone where the animal is and how big it is. Your call might help an otter like Eddie!

"Bring," she said. Eddie brought the ball to her hand.

"Good!" She flipped Eddie a yummy shrimp. She had him do it again, but this time, she held her hand higher. He had to reach higher to give her the ball. He pushed himself partway out of the water. When he put it into her hand, he got more treats!

Next, Jenny got a small, plastic hoop. She attached the logo of Oregon's National Basketball Association (NBA) team, the Portland Trail Blazers, on the backboard. She hung it above his training pool. It was two feet (61 cm) above the surface of the water. Jenny held her hand over the basket.

"Bring," she said. When he popped up to put it into her hand, she said "Basket."

Every time he did it right, Jenny threw him a tasty treat and praised him. Then she tossed the ball back to him. She did this over and over.

One day, she held her hand over the hoop and said "Basket." But she didn't take the ball like she always did. So Eddie dropped it. It went right through the hoop. *Two points!*

"Good!" she cried. This time she gave him a heap of treats. She wanted him to know that he had done something big. Over the next few days, she started to move her hand away from the hoop. She gave a hand signal, like shooting the ball with one hand. She did this a few times, saying his cue word, "Basket." She hoped he would take his best shot.

Slam dunk! That budding NBA player shot the ball into the basket. This time, he got a whole pile of his favorite shellfish.

Eddie shot hoops every day. He hardly ever missed. And if he did, he would try again without being asked. Eddie didn't do this to entertain zoo visitors. He wasn't in any kind of

> **Did You Know?**
>
> **The largest otter is the South American river otter. At six feet (1.8 m) long and 75 pounds (34 kg), it's the giant in the otter family!**

show. He did it in his private exercise pool to help his elbows. But one day, the zoo decided to make a video of Eddie playing basketball. It was so much fun to watch him. They posted it on the Internet. More than a million and a half people watched it. Everyone thought that Eddie was just the best! Watch out, Michael Jordan. Eddie might just be the biggest basketball superstar ever!

Suddenly, Eddie and Jenny were being interviewed by reporters. Jenny did all the talking. Eddie just hung out, looking cute. Their story was on the news around the country. The Portland Trail Blazers team even showed Eddie's video at a game!

Today, Eddie plays basketball regularly. When he's not shooting hoops, he hangs out with his best friend, Thelma. And he likes to play with the zoo's newest sea otter pup, Juno.

Sometimes the superstar sea otter likes to show off. Jenny gives Eddie a cue to "do something." That means he can perform whatever behavior he wants. It's a way to keep his mind active.

Sometimes he will spin. Sometimes he will open his mouth. But sometimes he has his own ideas. One day he swam to the side of the pool and took a pirate hat. He put it on his head. Then he swam around wearing it. *Arghhh, matey.* He had never been trained to do that— it was all his own idea! What will Eddie think of next?

Did You Know?

If humans needed to eat as much as otters, a 60-pound (27-kg) boy would have to eat 15 pounds (6.8 kg) a day. That's 60 quarter-pound hamburgers *every day!*

Look! No hands! Kidogo
walks a tightrope.

KIDOGO:
A BALANCING APE!

Kidogo leaps up to get a better view.

GOING APE

For hundreds of years, people have perfected the art of walking on high wires. Acrobats slide down slanted wires. Clowns juggle on loose ropes. Men and women tiptoe on tight wires strung between tall buildings. Tightrope walking is dangerous. It takes balance. It takes practice—unless you're Kidogo (sounds like kee-DOH-goh). He never had lessons. And he doesn't practice.

One day, Kidogo just held out his arms to his sides. Then he marched across a 13-foot (4-m) rope that was five and a half feet (1.7 m) off the ground. Who's Kidogo? He's a 440-pound (200-kg) gorilla!

Kidogo lives in a German zoo. He didn't always live there. He was born in a zoo in Denmark. Kidogo is a western gorilla. There are two kinds of gorillas—eastern and western. They look a lot alike. Eastern gorillas have longer, darker hair. Some of them live in the mountains. Western gorillas are a little smaller. They have longer arms and pointy heads. Most western gorillas live in rain forests.

There aren't many gorillas left in the wild. People hunted them. Their forests are shrinking. That makes life hard for gorillas. They need trees to live. They don't sleep in them. They snooze in nests on the ground. But they make their nests out of tree leaves. And they feast on nuts and fruit from trees.

Both eastern and western gorillas are shy and keep to themselves. The gorillas that live in zoos are western gorillas, like Kidogo.

Kidogo's father was born in the wild. He came from a country in western Africa. His name was Samson. Samson lived for many years in Denmark. When he was moved to a different zoo in Denmark, people took notice. Samson was a beautiful gorilla. Lots of people came to visit him at his new home.

One day, a special visitor arrived. Her name was Minnie. Minnie was a gorilla, too. She came from a zoo in France. She was to be Samson's new mate. About a year later, zookeepers learned that Minnie was going to have a baby. It would be her first baby. And it would be the first baby gorilla born at the zoo.

The zookeepers were very excited. Samson and Minnie had a son. The zoo named the baby Kidogo. That means "small" in the Swahili (sounds like swah-HEE-lee) language. What a strange name for a gorilla!

Of course, Kidogo was small when he was born. Newborn gorillas weigh between three and four pounds (1.4 and 1.8 kg). And he was so cute. Baby gorillas always are!

Baby Kidogo

Minnie was a careful mother. She fed her baby. She hugged him to her chest when she carried him. That's how gorilla mothers carry their newborn babies. When Kidogo was about three months old, Minnie lifted him onto her back. Kidogo wrapped his arms and legs around her. He held on tight. Over the next few months, Kidogo kept growing. Soon he would not need his mother's help to get around.

Monkeying Around

Monkeys and apes are both primates. But they are different. The most obvious difference is that most monkeys have tails. Some monkeys use their tails to help them climb. Another difference is size. Most monkeys are smaller than apes. Their noses are different, too. Monkeys have long snouts. That's because they use their sense of smell more than apes do. Apes are smarter than monkeys. Chimps and bonobos (sounds like buh-NOH-bohs) are very smart apes. They know how to use tools. They are able to solve problems.

The gorilla area in the Denmark zoo was big. There was plenty of room to play. Kidogo loved to roll over rocks and logs. He was athletic (sounds like ath-LEH-tik). He would be good at sports! Before long, more baby gorillas were born at the zoo. Soon Kidogo had six sisters and brothers to play with. Young gorillas play like human children. They wrestle (sounds like REH-suhl). They shove each other. They swing from branches. Sometimes they tickle each other. *Tee-hee!* Young gorillas even giggle!

Kidogo was very happy with his family. He was growing up. And he was growing curious. He was so curious that he sometimes got into trouble. The zoo built a fence around some of the smaller trees in the gorilla area. It was to protect them while they grew. One day, Kidogo figured out how to get behind the fence. He climbed to the top of a tree. But he was too heavy for the young tree. The tree bent. It bent all the way to the wall of the gorilla area. Kidogo hopped onto the wall. This athlete was ready for an adventure. He ran along the top of the wall. Maybe that's how he got his start as a tightrope walker. Next, he climbed onto the roof of the gorilla house.

The zookeepers saw him. Boy, were they upset. "Kidogo, Kidogo!" they yelled. They waved their arms at him.

Did You Know?

Until 1956, no gorilla had been born in captivity, like in a zoo. But on December 22, Colo was born at the Columbus Zoo in Ohio, U.S.A.

78

Kidogo stopped and looked at them. He leaped gracefully back onto the wall. He ran along it. *What would he do next? Would he jump out of the gorilla area?* The zookeepers held their breath. Luckily, he jumped back *into* the gorilla area! *Phew.*

That was his first escape. Another time, the zoo got a new female gorilla. Someone started a fight with her. The zookeepers thought it was Kidogo. So they put him in a time-out. Kidogo was upset. He yanked a large branch from a tree. He carried it to the gorilla house. He leaned it against the wall. Then he climbed up. *Uh-oh!*

Kidogo takes a look around his enclosure.

This time, Kidogo hopped off onto the *other* side of the wall. He had escaped from the gorilla area! Zoos build their gorilla areas carefully so that the gorillas rarely get out. But Kidogo was a rare gorilla. He was strong. And he liked challenges. He set out to explore the rest of the zoo. He strutted into the safari area. Antelope were grazing on grass.

He hadn't seen antelope before. He was curious. He headed toward them.

The antelope glanced up at the giant gorilla. They were scared. They ran around in circles. That scared Kidogo. He scampered up a tree.

Finally, the zookeepers caught up with him. They gave him some medicine to calm him down. He was so calm, he fell asleep. Then he fell out of the tree! It was 39 feet (12 m) tall. But that strong ape didn't even get hurt!

By now, Kidogo was almost grown up. A teenage male gorilla is called a blackback. When a blackback is around 12 years old, he changes. A patch of hair down his back turns silver. He becomes a silverback. And he wants to be in charge.

Gorillas live in families called troops. A gorilla troop can have several females and lots of children. There can be 30 gorillas in a troop. But there's only one silverback. The silverback tells the troop when it's time to move to a new place. He protects the troop. If he sees danger, the silverback stands up. He puffs himself up to look as big as possible. Sometimes he roars. Sometimes he throws things. Then he beats his chest. If that doesn't stop an animal, the silverback charges. Gorillas are usually gentle. But you don't want to get in the way of a charging 400-pound (181-kg) silverback!

When a blackback is 11 or 12 years old,

he's ready to leave the troop. He wants to make his own troop. Then he can be in charge. He leaves slowly. First, he heads out for a little walk. Then he comes home. He goes for little walks for several days, wandering a little farther each time he goes. But he still comes home. When he feels brave enough, he doesn't come back. Then he looks for a female to start a family.

Kidogo lived in a zoo. Blackbacks can't just walk out of a zoo. Not even Kidogo could do that! In a zoo, blackbacks are put in a separate area. Then the zoo finds a female or two. The blackback can start his new family. But sometimes a zoo doesn't have room to add a gorilla family. Then they send the blackback to another zoo.

Gorillas in the Mist

A young zoologist (sounds like zoh-AH-luh-jist) named Dian Fossey visited Uganda (sounds like yoo-GAHN-duh) in Africa. She fell in love with the mountain gorillas there. She studied them and learned about their behavior. She used their body language to show her respect. They let her sit with their troop. Her work helped us understand these gentle giants. She also worked to protect them from hunters. In 1988, a movie about her life was made. It was called *Gorillas in the Mist*.

The zoo in Denmark didn't have room for another family. They needed to find Kidogo a new home. The Krefeld (sounds like KREE-felt) Zoo is in Germany. It had just built a new gorilla area. It was called the Gorilla Garden. The Krefeld Zoo wanted to add gorillas. But their silverback couldn't have any more children. They moved him to a separate place. In the brand-new area, they had two young females, Muna and Oya. Now they just needed a young male gorilla.

Where can we find one? the director of the zoo wondered. Then he talked to someone at another zoo. That zoo had a list of all the gorillas in zoos around the world. They saw Kidogo's name on the list. The director and a zookeeper from the

Krefeld Zoo traveled to Denmark. They met Kidogo. He was big and strong. And most of all, he was athletic. *He's perfect,* thought the head of the zoo.

The German zookeeper got to know Kidogo. Then he found a gorilla-size wooden crate. He placed Kidogo's crate on a truck. He and Kidogo headed for Germany. But things didn't turn out like everyone thought they would.

You would think young Kidogo would have been excited in his new home. The Gorilla Garden was gigantic! It was 12,916 square feet (1,200 sq m). It had enough room for 10 gorillas! A creek ran through its hills. It had a meadow. There was even a termite mound! Gorillas don't usually eat meat. But they will chow down if they find tasty termites! In bad weather, the apes could go inside their very own villas.

But Kidogo was unhappy. The new zoo was a big change for the gorilla. It's kind of like moving to a new neighborhood. He was in a strange place. He didn't have any friends or family. Like people, gorillas can be nervous in new places. And they can be homesick.

Kidogo was a strong gorilla. But he had a soft heart. He missed his family. He didn't play with his new toys. He didn't climb on the ropes or platforms. He didn't go near the females. And he was shy around the zookeepers. Gorillas show their emotions with their faces and their bodies. They communicate with each other by small movements. A shrug or a stare can say a lot to a gorilla. One of the zookeepers thought he might be scared, too.

I think he's afraid that a silverback will come to fight him, he thought. So the zookeepers talked to Kidogo. They tried to get him to feel at home. One zookeeper was very fond of Kidogo. And Kidogo seemed to like her. Her name was Eva. She had a special nickname for Kidogo.

"Teddy Bear," she would say to him in German. "How are you today?" Of course, Kidogo never answered, but Eva felt sure he was listening.

Kidogo uses a rope to lift himself off the ground.

After a few weeks, Kidogo seemed to understand that the Gorilla Garden was all for him. No one was going to take it away. He calmed down. He tested out a few of his rope toys. The zookeepers noticed that his mouth was open when he played. That was a sign that he was content. He also paid attention to Muna and Oya. He understood that they were his mates.

Kidogo had always been a good athlete. One day, it rained hard. Then the sun came out. Kidogo ran outside. He turned somersault after somersault. Kidogo was himself again! Soon, he rumbled over rocks and logs. Sometimes he hauled himself up on a rope. He looked like he was doing pull-ups! And sometimes he jumped from the top of a 13-foot (4-m)-tall tree. He held his arms by his sides. And he landed on his feet. Maybe he was training for the Olympics!

The Gorilla Garden was next door to a soccer field. A German soccer team practiced there. Kidogo loved to watch soccer. Maybe he wanted to play soccer, too. Kidogo could probably kick a ball pretty far! *Goal!* Kidogo liked to watch other things, too. Sometimes visitors showed him movies. They held their tablets up to the glass. Kidogo was curious. He would sit and watch. He really liked animal videos.

He also liked to watch live rabbits. Kidogo chased wild rabbits when they came into the Gorilla Garden. *Boom, boom, boom!* He pounded the ground as he tracked them. But rabbits are very fast. He couldn't catch them. Then he would get mad. Like a spoiled child, he tossed tree roots around.

It's important to keep gorillas that live in zoos challenged so they don't get bored. So the zookeepers hid nuts in the garden.

Kidogo and the other gorillas hunted for these tasty treasures! And the zoo gave the gorillas food in plastic bags. The gorillas had to figure out how to open the bags to get the food out. Kidogo munched on all kinds of vegetables. He ate 22 pounds (10 kg) of food every day. In the summer, he found herbs (sounds like ERBS) in the garden. He gobbled them up. But his favorite food was peanuts.

The zookeepers put lots of ropes in the Gorilla Garden. The ropes were for exercise. Some of the ropes stretched from one wooden platform to another. The gorillas could swing on the ropes. Or they could hang from them. Or they climbed on them. But not Kidogo. That gorilla had other plans for the ropes.

Gorillas are strong. They have very long arms. They touch their arms to the ground when they walk. It's called knuckle walking. Gorillas can also stand up. They can walk on two feet for a little while. Zookeepers saw that Kidogo walked on two feet when he used his hands to carry food. But he walked standing up at other times, too. He walked on two feet more than most gorillas do.

One day, Kidogo was sitting on top of a tree trunk. He glanced around. He wanted to get to another part of the Gorilla Garden. So he stood up on two legs. He put one arm out to his side. He put the other arm over his head. He stepped onto a nearby rope. Without pausing, he gracefully tiptoed across the entire rope.

Primate Primer

Primates are mammals. What makes them so special? For one thing, primates are supersmart. And they can grab things with their hands and feet. They also see things in three dimensions. Monkeys are primates. Apes, like gorillas and chimps, are primates, too. So are humans. Humans have shorter arms than apes. And we walk on two feet all the time. But otherwise, humans and apes are a lot alike. The gorilla is our third closest cousin. Maybe that's why people like gorillas so much!

The zookeepers couldn't believe it. No one had ever heard of a gorilla walking on a tightrope. *How could a 440-pound (200-kg) gorilla balance like that?* they wondered. And he didn't even look down. Kidogo did it again. And again.

One day, a man was visiting the zoo. His job was to take interesting photographs. That day, as he watched, Kidogo stepped onto the rope. The photographer took Kidogo's picture. The zoo sent the picture out on a holiday email.

Soon the photo became famous. People around the world heard about the tightrope-walking ape. They wanted to see him for themselves. Lots of people went to the zoo to visit him. Overnight, his nickname went from "Teddy Bear" to "King Kodo!"

Experts on gorillas are surprised by what Kidogo does. He is a true athlete. He showed them how agile gorillas can be. He showed them something else, too. People may know a lot about gorillas. But we still have a lot to learn!

Kidogo is older now, but he's still athletic. Fame hasn't changed him. But being a father has. Kidogo seems to like being a dad. He now has two sons— Tambo and Pepe. Tambo was born in the summer of 2013. When a gorilla is around two years old, he starts learning about being a gorilla from his father. Kidogo spends a lot of time with his sons. Maybe he'll teach them how to tightrope walk. Or maybe, like their dad, they'll teach themselves!

THE END

DON'T MISS!

NATIONAL GEOGRAPHIC KiDS · CHAPTERS

TOGETHER FOREVER!

True Stories of Amazing Animal Friendships!

Mary Quattlebaum

Turn the page
for a sneak preview . . .

Penny is a chicken. Roo is a dog. They became fast friends.

PENNY AND ROO:
ON THE
MOVE!

Penny and Roo met at the Duluth Animal Hospital in Georgia, U.S.A. They've been attached ever since.

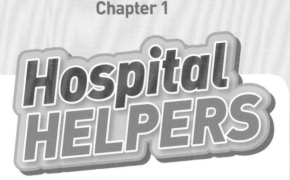

Hospital HELPERS

Dogs strain at their leashes. Cats meow in their carriers. A fluffy chicken scampers by in a diaper. Then a tiny dog wheels past in a special cart. The front desk of the Duluth Animal Hospital is busy! Many animals are brought here if they're sick or injured. The veterinarians (sounds like vet-er-ih-NAIR-ee-enz) here treat all kinds of animals.

Their patients include dogs, cats, hamsters, lizards, turtles, even chickens. They help their animal patients feel better or give them shots to keep them from getting sick.

But the chicken and the little dog—called a Chihuahua (sounds like chi-WAH-wah)—aren't patients. Penny and Roo work here. These two best friends welcome animal patients and their owners to the hospital in Duluth, Georgia, U.S.A.

The hospital staff appreciates their good work, especially Alicia Williams, their owner. Alicia works here as a receptionist. She helps patients prepare for their visit with the vets. So do Penny and Roo. Sometimes the patients are frightened or in pain. Their owners are worried.

But then Penny does something silly. She steals Roo's treat and trots fast, fast, fast on her feathered legs. Roo chases her and tries to grab the treat back. People smile and laugh. The two friends are so funny that they help everyone—animals and humans—feel more relaxed.

Penny and Roo have been working together for three and a half years. How did these two unique friends get this special job? Penny came first. Alicia met Penny when she was taking a class in animal science. Alicia had to learn about what happens when animals are used in research, and she had to visit some places that did this work.

Research is an important way to learn more about both animals and humans.

Here's how it works. Scientists study a small group of research animals. They give the animals in the group a special diet or medicine. Then they carefully observe, or watch for, changes in the animals. Do the animals grow bigger? Do they get better?

The scientists gather the information. They write papers about what they have learned and publish them. Other people can read about their research and learn how to improve the food they grow or the medicine they make or give. Scientists and doctors often learn about the effect of certain medicines on humans by looking at how the medicines affect animals.

Penny was a research animal in a study on diet. Alicia saw her on the last day of the study. Now that the research was done, the scientists would no longer need her.

Alicia looked at the young chicken. Penny was a beautiful hen! Instead of smooth feathers like most birds, hers were soft and fluffy. The feathers on her head and legs looked like a puffy hat and pants. Alicia wanted to give the hen a new home. "May I have her?" she asked the researchers.

And that's how Alicia ended up bringing Penny to the house she shares with her parents, three sisters, five dogs, two cats, and four parrots. Everyone in Alicia's family is an animal lover!

At first, Alicia didn't know how to care for Penny. Parrots and chickens are both birds, but they require different care.

Fancy Feathers

Silkies are unique chickens, with soft, silky feathers. They have black bones and black skin. They don't look very much like the jungle fowl that all chickens are descended from. One of their distant ancestors is the *Tyrannosaurus rex!* Silkies have some special traits. They have five toes instead of the usual four, and they have blue earlobes. They can't fly. Silkies like to brood, or sit on their eggs. They will even hatch the eggs of other birds.

Penny was also not a regular chicken. She was a fancy, gentle type called a silkie.

Alicia's boss, Dr. Mike Miller, was very helpful. He's a veterinarian. He told Alicia that chickens need special food and plenty of time outdoors. Alicia made Penny an outdoor pen so that she could scratch at the ground and search for bugs and seeds to eat.

But because Penny is very friendly, Alicia also made her an indoor pen. Chickens are flock animals and like to be with other chickens. With an indoor pen, Penny could be around the other pets and people in the house.

Penny quickly settled into her new . . .

Want to know what happens next? Be sure to check out *Together Forever!* Available wherever books and ebooks are sold.

INDEX

Boldface indicates illustrations.

MORE INFORMATION

To find out more information about the animals mentioned in this book, check out the links below.

Norman's website
normanthescooterdog .com

Oregon Zoo, home of Eddie
oregonzoo.org

"Sea Otter Hoop Dreams"
youtube.com/ watch?v=cJTRCtwf_X0

National Geographic Kids "Sea Otter"
kids.nationalgeographic.com/ animals/sea-otter/#sea -otter-closeup2.jpg

Krefeld Zoo, home of Kidogo
zookrefeld.de/en.html

National Geographic "Lowland Gorilla"
animals.nationalgeographic .com/animals/mammals/ lowland-gorilla

Dian Fossey Gorilla Fund
gorillafund.org

CREDITS

For Eileen and Laurie, fabulous friends and
my favorite librarians. — MRD

ACKNOWLEDGMENTS

My special thanks go to the following people:

The team at National Geographic: Brenna Maloney, my
magical editor with a wicked sense of humor; Shelby Alinsky,
the most gracious and amazing project manager; researcher
extraordinaire Kathryn Williams; and the entire design team.

Karen Cobb, for generously sharing the story of Norman, her
superstar dog.

Jenny DeGroot and Hova Najarian of the Oregon Zoo, for their
thoroughness and diligence in telling Eddie's special tale.

Petra Schwinn of the Krefeld Zoo and Richard Østerballe of
the Givskud Zoo, for their willingness to provide a wealth of
information about Kidogo in a short time and IN ENGLISH!

Dr. Tara Stoinski, CEO of the Dian Fossey Gorilla Fund, for her
helpful insights into the mind of the amazing Kidogo.

And, as always, my supportive family.